A Guide to the

SCIENCE KID

Author: DANIEL D. WARREN

A Guide to the SCIENCE KID

Books for kids

By: Daniel D. Warren

First Printing, 2022

Disclaimer

The publisher and author make no representation or warranties with respect to the accuracy of the book contents and specifically disclaim all warrants, including warranties of fitness for a particular reason. If professional assistance needed, the service should be sought out.

The Story

I am Kymani. I was born into a family of four.

My father works at the hospital, while my mother owns a grocery store.

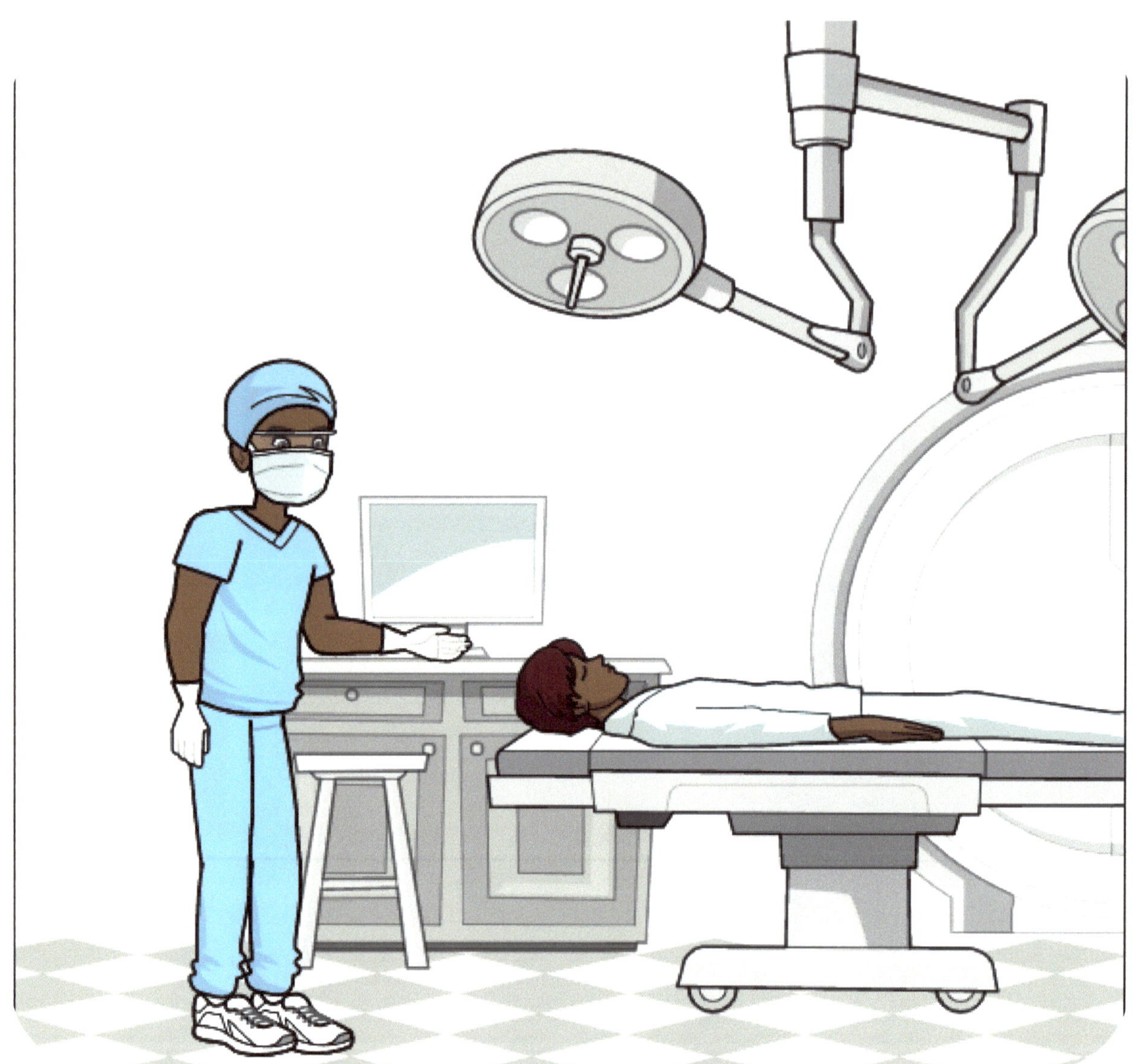

As an elder brother, I am always instructed to babysit my little brother, Andrew, who is only 2 years old, and I am 15. While babysitting, I discovered some strange things my younger brother is fond of.

Kids carry out their own experiments too. Funny, isn't it? Yes, and these explorations are weird.

Sometimes, I wonder if I also performed those kinds of research when I was younger.

On a faithful Sunday mid-afternoon, Dad was at work, and mom decided I should stay at home as she was attending an important ceremony.

I was left with Andrew.

I love watching movies, especially Japanese action series, so I was on the sitting room couch, focusing my attention on the flat screen.

After a long stare at the TV, it came to my mind that there was no noise. Everything was as silent as a graveyard except for the noise of the foreign language coming out of the TV.

I stood up, hoping to hear at least a different sound than the one from my Japanese film.

With that, I discovered a sound like the opening and closing of a door, so I moved immediately, hoping to locate Andrew.

As I got to him, he was with the smaller fridge. The strangest and funniest thing was that he held the fridge door closer to his eyes, staring at the bulb inside and slowly closing the door, hoping to see how the bulb would go off.

Normally, each time Mom goes to the fridge with him and opens it, the light is always off but immediately turns on after a few seconds as she opens it. But as she closes it, the lights are always on until it closes completely. I guess the question on his mind as a kid was, "How does it go off?"

"Andrew! What are you doing there?" I spoke to him. Immediately, he looked at me and was frightened because I had come near him without him noticing.

He giggled, "Yes!

Andrew burst into excitement as he pointed to the fridge, saying "Yes" to it while looking at me. "Yes" is one of the words he can say as he is too young. He answers most questions with yes.

Kids are the weirdest scientist in the world, aren't they? Just kidding.

One sunny afternoon after school, I went out to take Andrew from school as I was the only one available. Mom was busy with our business in her store while dad was at the hospital.

We were at home, and I turned on the television for Andrew so he could carry on with cartoons. He gets excited when it's time to watch his "PJ mask," a fictional animated series he is fond of.

As he watched, there was a spark, and the light and TV went off. The enthusiasm in Andrew went away. He hates it when there is a power outage. Immediately, he went to the TV. What surprised me was that he took a stool to check if the characters displayed on the TV were still available inside. He held a torch pointing inside while staring at the internal components like a professional engineer.

These acts are so strange but are truly worth complimenting. Every kid is a scientist exploring their journey to become what they don't know yet.

This is a gift like no other.

David & the marvelous metal Basket

My name is David, and I was born into a nuclear family. My sister, my mom, dad and I.

My sister's name is Mary, who is four levels ahead of me.

My parents' names are Mrs. Jackie Michael and Mr. John Michael.

I'm only eight years old and about three feet tall, and I attend the John Rowe primary school..

My mum and dad are both primary school teachers. My mum takes good care of us.

Early in the morning, before going to school, I always have a fresh bath and brushed my teeth. My mom would say that my sister and I should pray for at least a minute before going to school.

As a family, we both shared the same interest and pleasure in sports; our favorite sport is disc golf.

Playing the disc golf game is very simple and very similar to golf. Just follow the course's numbered holes. Initiate your first throw from the starting pad, then play from wherever your disc lands. Each hole has a par (typically anywhere from 2 to 5), and so the lower your score, the better. Playing the game involves the use of a spare ball, bug spray, a basket, etc.

We had just moved into our newly purchased apartments in Cape Town, where we had a wide and long field at the main front of our house for us to play our disc golf game. To us, playing disc golf games is everything that is worth joy and excitement. When things go wrong at home, the importance of playing the game brings love and peace into the home.

We had a lot of fun playing disc golf together, especially on weekends.

My first attempt at learning the disc golf game was at age 5, what created my love and passion for the game was the pleasure of kicking off the spare ball and holding the basket. I am always attracted to the basket.

Every day when I get home from school, my father teaches me how to play disc golf.

Learning how to play the game is fun. Just as I started learning the game of disc golf, my knowledge and intellectual style of learning increased my studies in my life and work.

(The disc golf game is excellent for instilling love in others and increasing the brain's sense of intelligence.)

During the summer, our school principal organized a disc golf-themed recreational sport activity for all students on the school grounds.

I would train with my family. My sister , mum dad and I, at our new house.

Coming back early from school on Fridays, my family and I will play disc golf together after taking our breakfast until night falls.

While playing the game, we form groups and teams together. My sister would always love to be with Dad, and I always love playing with my mum.

Mary: Dad! "Pass the ball to me."

Mr. John: "Ok, I will

David: "Mum, let's take a guide for our goal pole."

"Yes, okay," Mrs. Jackie says.

It is a lot of fun and very entertaining.

Today is Monday and it is back to school, oh yeah. It was a sunny day.

A tournament will be held between both classes. My class is A, while our opposing team is Class B.

As we were about to begin my friend and I formed a team. It was exciting, and we enjoyed playing the game, at our final tournament.

I learned and trained with my family, which helped me to be able to catch up faster with other pupils in the school, so that we could win the competition.

My class had made it to the final level and it now time for the final tournament to begin.

My class teacher is our coach. All students are present at the school field to watch the game until it end.

The game begins, It is tough for us to win the game.

All the training with my parents has given me the confidence to win. The game lasted four hours and forty-five minutes.

Two hours passed and the game became more interesting. My mum and sister were present; they watched us play the game, expecting a good performance from me.

We had scored seven goals by the end of the game, while our opponents scores only one.

The game was over, and our class team won. We fell fantastic winning the tournament.

There was a celebration for our class as the winners of the tournament. Being the overall winner, we received gold medals.

With the help of my family , I was able to assist my team in winning the disc golf tournament.

THE END

About the Author

Daniel Warren is a student of the Mineral Heights Primary School in Jamaica. He is the Author of:

Daniel's Bedtime Stories

A Cat for Santa

The Science Kid

These books are a great introduction for readers of all experience levels. Your child will be captivated by this story, which entails simple language and attractive illustrations for young readers.

The story talks about kymani and his little two-year-old brother, Andrew, who is fond of carrying out amazing experiments. Kymani' s mother works at a grocery store while his father is a medical doctor.

Each day Kymani is left alone to babysit his little brother, he always finds Andrew carrying out a certain experiment. Kymani always imagines what kind of experiment his little brother is up to. Kymani' s act of experimenting shows his great talents and pictures his future.

It' s time to sleep, little one.

www.ingramcontent.com/pod-product-compliance
Lightning Source LLC
LaVergne TN
LVHW071111160826
845679LV00004B/1040

* 9 7 9 8 3 7 0 4 6 5 6 8 0 *